From Unemployment to Entrepreneurship: A Guide to Starting Your Own Business

Asit Saha

Published by Asit Saha, 2024.

While every precaution has been taken in the preparation of this book, the publisher assumes no responsibility for errors or omissions, or for damages resulting from the use of the information contained herein.

FROM UNEMPLOYMENT TO ENTREPRENEURSHIP: A GUIDE TO STARTING YOUR OWN BUSINESS

First edition. April 4, 2024.

ISBN: 979-8224304127

Written by Asit Saha.

Overview

In today's rapidly evolving economic landscape, the journey from unemployment to entrepreneurship has become increasingly common—and remarkably transformative. "From Unemployment to Entrepreneurship" offers a comprehensive roadmap for individuals navigating this transition, providing practical guidance, inspirational insights, and actionable strategies to turn adversity into opportunity.

Through this book, readers will embark on a transformative journey, guided by a structured approach that empowers them to unleash their entrepreneurial potential. Beginning with an exploration of personal skills, interests, and passions, the book guides readers through the process of identifying viable business ideas and crafting a compelling vision for their ventures. From creating a robust business plan to navigating legal and regulatory requirements, readers will gain the knowledge and confidence to lay a solid foundation for their businesses.

Financial considerations are a critical aspect of entrepreneurship, and this book offers practical advice on budgeting, funding options, and financial management during the startup phase. Moreover, it demystifies legal and regulatory complexities, providing clear guidance on business structures, registrations, licenses, and intellectual property protection.

Building a strong brand and developing compelling products or services are crucial steps towards entrepreneurial success. This book equips readers with strategies for branding, marketing, and product development, drawing from real-world examples and case studies to illustrate best practices and pitfalls to avoid.

Launching a business is a pivotal moment in the entrepreneurial journey, and this book offers insights into generating buzz, attracting customers, and managing the initial growth phase. Moreover, it addresses common challenges faced by entrepreneurs and provides practical advice for overcoming obstacles with resilience and determination.

As readers progress on their entrepreneurial journey, the book explores strategies for scaling and sustaining business growth, empowering them to achieve their long-term goals and aspirations. Through a blend of practical guidance, inspirational stories, and actionable insights, "From Unemployment to Entrepreneurship" serves as a trusted companion for individuals embarking on the path to entrepreneurial success in today's dynamic business landscape.

Chapters

Chapter 1: Introduction

Chapter1: Introduction

In the wake of unexpected job loss, the uncertainty of unemployment can be overwhelming. Yet, amidst the challenges lie hidden opportunities—ones that can lead to thoughtful personal and professional growth. It's within this period of transition that the concept of starting a business after unemployment emerges, offering a beacon of hope and a pathway to a new chapter.

The journey from unemployment to entrepreneurship is more than a mere career shift; it's a transformational odyssey characterized by resilience, innovation, and unwavering determination. It's a journey that begins with introspection and ends with the creation of something meaningful—a business that not only sustains livelihoods but also fulfills dreams and aspirations.

At its core, the concept of starting a business after unemployment embodies the spirit of adaptability and resourcefulness. It's about leveraging one's skills, experiences, and passions to create value in the marketplace, even amidst adversity. It's about embracing uncertainty as an opportunity for growth and embracing failure as a stepping stone to success.

Throughout this book, we'll delve into the intricacies of this transformative journey, offering practical guidance, inspirational insights, and actionable strategies for aspiring entrepreneurs. From identifying business ideas to crafting a compelling vision, from navigating legal complexities to overcoming challenges, we'll explore every facet of the entrepreneurial landscape.

But perhaps most importantly, we'll celebrate the indomitable human spirit—the resilience that propels individuals to rise from the ashes of unemployment and forge their own paths toward success. So, whether you find yourself at a crossroads or on the brink of a new beginning, know that the journey from unemployment to entrepreneurship is not just a leap of faith—it's a journey of empowerment, growth, and endless possibilities. Welcome to the adventure.

Allow me to share a personal anecdote that illustrates the transformative power of entrepreneurship after experiencing unemployment:

Several years ago, I found myself in the unsettling position of being unexpectedly laid off from my corporate job. In an instant, the stability I had grown accustomed to be replaced with uncertainty and doubt. Despite my initial shock and dismay, I soon realized that this unexpected setback presented an opportunity—a chance to redefine my career on my own terms.

Embracing the uncertainty, I embarked on a journey of self-discovery and exploration, delving into my passions and uncovering hidden talents I never knew I possessed. As I reflected on my experiences and aspirations, a spark of entrepreneurial spirit ignited within me—a desire to create something meaningful and impactful, not just for myself, but for others as well.

Drawing upon my background in marketing and a lifelong passion for sustainability, I launched a small consulting firm focused on helping eco-conscious businesses thrive in a competitive market. It wasn't easy navigating the challenges of entrepreneurship—there were moments of doubt, setbacks, and sleepless nights. Yet, with each obstacle, I grew stronger and more determined to succeed.

One of the most rewarding aspects of this journey has been the opportunity to connect with like-minded individuals who share my vision for a more sustainable future. Whether collaborating with passionate entrepreneurs or inspiring others to pursue their own dreams, every interaction reaffirms my belief in the power of entrepreneurship to effect positive change in the world.

Today, as I reflect on my journey from unemployment to entrepreneurship, I am filled with gratitude for the lessons learned, the connections made, and the impact created. While the path may have been winding and challenging at times, I wouldn't trade it for anything. For in the end, it's not just about the destination—it's about the journey, the growth, and the transformation that comes from daring to pursue your dreams against all odds.

Chapter 2: Assessing The Situation

Reflecting on the experience of unemployment brings forth a myriad of emotions and challenges that many can relate to. It's a period characterized by uncertainty, stress, and a sense of loss—loss of routine, identity, and financial stability. Yet, amidst the turmoil, there's also an opportunity for introspection, growth, and resilience.

Personally, the experience of unemployment was a profound wake-up call—a stark reminder of the fragility of stability and the unpredictable nature of life. As someone who had always prided themselves on their work ethic and dedication, being suddenly thrust into unemployment felt like a blow to my sense of self-worth and identity. The routine that had once anchored my days was replaced with a disorienting void, leaving me grappling with feelings of inadequacy and self-doubt.

Financially, the impact was palpable. With bills to pay and responsibilities to meet, the looming specter of financial insecurity cast a shadow over every decision and action. The stress of job hunting, coupled with the fear of dwindling savings, created a pervasive sense of anxiety that seemed to permeate every aspect of my life.

Yet, amidst the darkness, there were glimmers of light—moments of clarity and insight that emerged from the depths of uncertainty. It was during this period of unemployment that I was forced to confront uncomfortable truths about myself and my career aspirations. I began to question the conventional notion of success and reevaluate what truly mattered to me in life.

In retrospection, the experience of unemployment served as a catalyst for personal growth and introspection. It forced me to confront my fears, embrace vulnerability, and cultivate resilience in the face of adversity. It was a humbling reminder of the impermanence of life and the importance of adapting to change with grace and courage.

Adaptability and Resilience:

In the fast-paced world of entrepreneurship, adaptability and resilience are essential traits. Entrepreneurs must be prepared to pivot quickly in response to changing market conditions, setbacks, or unforeseen challenges. This involves maintaining a positive attitude, learning from failures, and bouncing back stronger than before.

Long-Term Vision and Goal Setting:

While employees may focus on short-term tasks and objectives, entrepreneurs adopt a long-term perspective, envisioning the future trajectory of their businesses. This mindset shift involves setting ambitious goals, developing strategic plans, and staying focused on the bigger picture, even in the face of immediate obstacles.

Self-Reliance and Continuous Learning: Entrepreneurs rely on their own resourcefulness and initiative to drive their ventures forward. This involves seeking out new opportunities, acquiring new skills, and continuously learning and adapting to stay ahead in a competitive landscape.

Embracing Failure as a Learning Opportunity:

Unlike the fear of failure that may permeate employee mindset, entrepreneurs view failure as a natural part of the learning process. They understand that each setback offers valuable lessons and insights that can ultimately lead to greater success.

Passion and Purpose-Driven Motivation:

Perhaps most importantly, the mindset shift from employee to entrepreneur is fueled by passion and purpose. Entrepreneurs are driven by a deep sense of passion for their work and a desire to make a meaningful impact on the world around them. This intrinsic motivation serves as a powerful force driving them forward, even in the face of adversity.

Chapter 3: Finding Your Business Idea

Generating business ideas can be a creative and dynamic process. Here are several methods to explore:

Identify Problems and Pain Points: Look for common problems or inconveniences that people face in their daily lives. Solutions to these problems can form the basis of a successful business. For example, if there's a lack of efficient transportation options in your area, consider starting a ride-sharing service.

Follow Your Passion and Skills: Consider your interests, hobbies, and skills. What are you passionate about? What are you good at? Often, businesses that align with your passions and skills have a higher chance of success because you'll be motivated to work on them consistently.

Market Research: Conduct thorough market research to identify gaps or underserved areas in the market. Analyze trends, consumer preferences, and competitors to find opportunities. Tools like surveys, focus groups, and online research can help gather valuable insights.

Observe Trends: Stay updated on current trends in various industries. Trends can provide valuable inspiration for new business ideas. Keep an eye on emerging technologies, societal shifts, and consumer behavior changes.

Brainstorming Sessions: Organize brainstorming sessions with friends, colleagues, or fellow entrepreneurs. Encourage open-mindedness and creativity. Write down all ideas, no matter how wild they may seem initially, and then evaluate them later for feasibility and potential.

SWOT Analysis: Conduct a SWOT (Strengths, Weaknesses, Opportunities, Threats) analysis of different industries or market segments. This can help you identify potential business ideas by assessing the strengths and weaknesses of existing businesses and finding areas where you could offer something unique.

Customer Feedback: Talk to potential customers to understand their needs, preferences, and pain points. Their feedback can spark ideas for products or services that address specific problems or fulfill unmet needs.

Franchise Opportunities: Investigate franchise opportunities in industries that interest you. Franchises provide a proven business model and support from the franchisor, which can be advantageous for first-time entrepreneurs.

Social and Environmental Issues: Consider starting a business that addresses social or environmental issues. Sustainable and socially responsible businesses are gaining popularity and can attract customers who prioritize ethical consumption.

Adapt Existing Ideas: Take existing business concepts and adapt or improve upon them. Look for areas where you can innovate or add value to differentiate your business from competitors.

Conduct market research and identify opportunities

Conducting market research is a crucial step in identifying opportunities for your business. Here's a roadmap on how to effectively conduct market research and pinpoint potential opportunities:

Define Your Objectives: Before diving into research, clarify your objectives. What specific information are you seeking? Are you looking to understand consumer preferences, assess market size, or identify competitors? Clearly defining your goals will guide your research efforts.

Identify Your Target Audience: Determine who your target customers are. What are their demographics, behaviors, and preferences? Understanding your target audience will help you tailor your research and identify opportunities that resonate with them.

Utilize Secondary Research: Start by gathering existing data and information from secondary sources such as industry reports, market studies, government publications, and academic journals. These sources can provide valuable insights into market trends, customer demographics, and competitor analysis.

Conduct Primary Research: Supplement secondary research with primary research to gather firsthand information. Primary research methods include surveys, interviews, focus groups, and observation. Engage with potential customers to understand their needs, pain points, and purchasing behaviors.

Assess Market Size and Growth: Determine the size and growth rate of your target market. Is the market expanding, contracting, or stagnant? Analyze historical data and future projections to gauge the market's potential for growth and opportunity.

Identify Competitors: Identify direct and indirect competitors operating in your target market. Analyze their products, pricing strategies, distribution channels, and marketing tactics. Understanding competitor strengths and weaknesses can help you identify gaps and opportunities in the market.

Evaluate Industry Trends: Stay updated on industry trends, technological advancements, regulatory changes, and consumer preferences. Analyze how these trends may impact your business and identify opportunities to capitalize on emerging trends or fill unmet needs.

SWOT Analysis: Conduct a SWOT analysis (Strengths, Weaknesses, Opportunities, Threats) to assess your business's internal strengths and weaknesses, as well as external opportunities and threats in the market. Identify areas where you can leverage your strengths to capitalize on opportunities and mitigate potential threats.

Explore Niche Markets: Consider exploring niche markets or underserved segments within your industry. Niche markets often present opportunities for businesses to establish themselves as experts or leaders in specialized areas and cater to specific customer needs.

Stay Flexible and Adapt: Market research is an ongoing process. Stay flexible and be prepared to adapt your strategies based on new information, changing market conditions, and evolving customer preferences. Continuously monitor market trends and customer feedback to identify new opportunities and refine your business approach.

Success stories of entrepreneurs who started businesses after unemployment

Highlighting success stories of entrepreneurs who started businesses after experiencing unemployment can provide inspiration and motivation for aspiring entrepreneurs. Here are a few examples:

JK Rowling:

Before becoming one of the most successful authors in the world, JK Rowling faced unemployment and financial struggles. She wrote the script for "Harry Potter and the Philosopher's Stone" while living on welfare benefits as a single mother. Despite facing numerous rejections from publishers, Rowling persisted and eventually found success. Her Harry Potter series became a global phenomenon, selling millions of copies worldwide and inspiring a successful film franchise.

Colonel Harland Sanders (KFC):

Colonel Harland Sanders, the founder of Kentucky Fried Chicken (KFC), faced a series of setbacks and failures throughout his life, including being fired from multiple jobs and experiencing financial difficulties. In his 60s, after retiring from his job as a gas station operator, Sanders started selling fried chicken from his roadside restaurant in Kentucky. His secret recipe and unique cooking method gained popularity, leading to the establishment of the KFC franchise, which has since become one of the largest fast-food chains in the world.

Vera Wang:

Vera Wang, a renowned fashion designer, began her career as a figure skater and later worked as a fashion editor at Vogue magazine. After being passed over for the editor-in-chief position, Wang was laid off from Vogue at the age of 40. Undeterred, she pursued her passion for fashion design and launched her own bridal wear company. Despite facing skepticism and financial challenges, Wang's designs gained recognition for their elegance and sophistication, making her a prominent figure in the fashion industry.

Chris Gardner:

Chris Gardner's story of going from homelessness to becoming a successful entrepreneur and motivational speaker is well-known. After struggling with homelessness and financial instability while raising his young son, Gardner entered a stockbroker training program. Despite facing numerous obstacles and setbacks, including sleeping in homeless shelters, Gardner persevered and eventually became a successful stockbroker and entrepreneur. His inspirational story was later depicted in the film "The Pursuit of Happyness," starring Will Smith.

Arianna Huffington:

Arianna Huffington, the co-founder of The Huffington Post, faced rejection and setbacks early in her career. After facing numerous rejections from publishers for her second book, Huffington experienced financial difficulties and was forced to leave her apartment. Undeterred, she continued to pursue her passion for writing and eventually co-founded The Huffington Post, a highly successful online news platform that was later acquired by AOL for $315 million.

These success stories demonstrate that facing unemployment or adversity does not have to define one's future. With determination, resilience, and a willingness to take risks, individuals can overcome challenges and achieve success as entrepreneurs.

Chapter 4: Creating a Business Plan

A business plan serves as a roadmap for your business, outlining your objectives, strategies, and action plans to achieve your goals. Here are several key reasons why formulating a business plan is important:

Clarifies Business Concept and Objectives:

A business plan helps you clarify your business concept and define your objectives. It forces you to articulate your business idea, target market, products or services, and unique value proposition. By clearly defining your goals, you can stay focused and aligned with your vision for the business.

Sets Direction and Goals:

A business plan sets the direction for your business and establishes measurable goals and milestones. It helps you identify what you want to achieve and how you plan to get there. By setting specific, achievable goals, you can track your progress and make informed decisions to move your business forward.

Attracts Investors and Funding:

A well-written business plan is essential for attracting investors, lenders, or potential partners. Investors want to see a clear and comprehensive plan that demonstrates the viability and potential of your business. A business plan helps instill confidence in stakeholders by showcasing your understanding of the market, competitive landscape, and growth opportunities.

Guides Decision-Making:

A business plan serves as a guide for decision-making and helps you anticipate challenges and opportunities. It provides a framework for evaluating different strategies and making informed choices based on data and analysis. Whether it's entering new markets, launching new products, or allocating resources, a business plan helps you make decisions that align with your long-term objectives.

Facilitates Resource Allocation:

A business plan helps you allocate resources effectively by outlining your budget, financial projections, and resource requirements. It helps you identify the funding needed to start and grow your business, as well as the anticipated revenue streams and expenses. By having a clear understanding of your financial needs, you can better manage cash flow, minimize risks, and optimize resource allocation.

Provides a Roadmap for Growth:

A business plan provides a roadmap for growth and expansion, outlining strategies for scaling your business over time. It helps you identify opportunities for diversification, partnerships, or market expansion. By regularly reviewing and updating your business plan, you can adapt to changing market conditions and seize new opportunities for growth.

Enhances Accountability and Monitoring:

A business plan enhances accountability by establishing targets and performance metrics that can be tracked and monitored over time. It helps you measure progress against your goals and identify areas where adjustments may be needed. By regularly reviewing key performance indicators (KPIs) and comparing them to your business plan, you can identify strengths and weaknesses and make necessary adjustments to stay on track.

A step-by-step guide to creating a comprehensive plan

Creating a comprehensive business plan involves several key steps. Here's a step-by-step guide to help you develop a thorough and effective business plan:

Executive Summary:

Start with an executive summary that provides an overview of your business concept, objectives, and key highlights of the plan. This section should grab the reader's attention and provide a snapshot of what the business is about.

Business Description:

Provide a detailed description of your business, including its mission, vision, values, and legal structure (e.g., sole proprietorship, partnership, LLC). Explain what sets your business apart from competitors and how you plan to fulfill unmet needs in the market.

Market Analysis:

Conduct a comprehensive analysis of your target market, including demographics, size, trends, and growth potential. Identify your target customers and their needs, preferences, and purchasing behaviors. Analyze the competitive landscape and assess the strengths, weaknesses, opportunities, and threats (SWOT) facing your business.

Marketing and Sales Strategy:

Outline your marketing and sales strategies for attracting and retaining customers. Describe your product or service offerings, pricing strategy, distribution channels, and promotional tactics. Define your sales process and customer acquisition strategy, including how you plan to generate leads and convert them into paying customers.

Operations and Management Plan:

Detail the operational and management structure of your business. Describe the day-to-day operations, key processes, and facilities or equipment needed to run the business. Identify key personnel and their roles and responsibilities, including management team members and any external advisors or consultants.

Product or Service Development:

If applicable, provide details about your product or service development process. Describe the features, benefits, and unique selling points of your offerings. Outline any research and development activities, intellectual property protections, and plans for future product or service enhancements.

Financial Projections:

Set up detailed financial projections, including income statements, cash flow statements, and balance sheets. Estimate your startup costs, ongoing expenses, and revenue projections for the first three to five years of operation. Use realistic assumptions and financial models to justify your projections and demonstrate the financial viability of your business.

Funding Request:

If you're seeking funding or investment, clearly state your funding requirements and how the funds will be used. Provide information about any existing funding or contributions from founders or investors. Describe your preferred funding sources (e.g., loans, equity investment) and the terms you're seeking.

Appendices:

Include any additional information or supporting documents that are relevant to your business plan, such as market research reports, resumes of key team members, legal documents, and contracts. Keep these materials organized and easily accessible for reference.

Review and Revision:

Review your business plan thoroughly to ensure accuracy, clarity, and coherence. Seek feedback from advisors, mentors, or other stakeholders, and incorporate any suggestions or revisions as needed. Regularly update your business plan as your business evolves and market conditions change.

The next question is how to structure your business plan? Look at these templates and examples to keep everything in grip.

Executive Summary:

Template: A concise overview of your business, including its mission, objectives, target market, unique value proposition, and financial highlights.

Example: "XYZ Company is a startup that aims to revolutionize the online grocery delivery industry by offering a convenient, affordable, and personalized shopping experience. Our platform connects customers with local grocery stores and independent vendors, providing same-day delivery and exclusive deals. With a projected revenue of $1 million in the first year, we are seeking $500,000 in funding to support our launch and expansion efforts."

Business Description:

Template: A detailed description of your business concept, products or services, target market, competitive advantage, and legal structure.

Example: "XYZ Company is a tech startup based in [Location] that specializes in developing AI-powered chatbots for customer service automation. Our proprietary technology enables businesses to streamline customer interactions, reduce response times, and improve overall efficiency. With a team of experienced software engineers and a strong focus on innovation, we are poised to disrupt the customer service industry and capture a significant market share."

Market Analysis:

Template: An analysis of your target market, including demographics, market size, trends, competition, and SWOT analysis.

Example: "The market for AI-powered chatbots is rapidly expanding, driven by the growing demand for automation solutions in various industries. According to market research firm Gartner, the global market for chatbots is expected to reach $1.25 billion by 2025, with a compound annual growth rate of 24%. Despite the presence of established players such as [Competitor 1] and [Competitor 2], there is still significant room for innovation and market penetration."

Marketing and Sales Strategy:

Template: A plan for attracting and retaining customers, including product/service offerings, pricing strategy, distribution channels, and promotional tactics.

Example: "XYZ Company will adopt a multi-channel marketing approach to reach our target audience, including social media advertising, content marketing, email campaigns, and partnerships with industry influencers. We will leverage data analytics and customer feedback to optimize our marketing efforts and maximize ROI. Additionally, we will offer competitive pricing packages and incentives to incentivize customer acquisition and retention."

Operations and Management Plan:

Template: Details about your operational processes, management structure, key personnel, and facilities/equipment requirements.

Example: "XYZ Company will operate as a lean startup, with a focus on agility, innovation, and scalability. Our core team consists of seasoned professionals with expertise in software development, artificial intelligence, and business strategy. We will utilize cloud-based infrastructure and agile methodologies to streamline development processes and adapt to changing market dynamics. Our office space will be located in [Location] and equipped with state-of-the-art technology to support our team's productivity and collaboration."

Financial Projections:

Template: Projections for startup costs, revenue, expenses, and cash flow over a three to five-year period.

Example: "Based on our market research and financial analysis, we anticipate generating $500,000 in revenue in our first year of operation, with a gross margin of 60%. Our projected expenses include personnel costs, marketing expenses, research and development, and overhead expenses, totaling $300,000. With an initial investment of $200,000, we expect to achieve profitability by the end of the second year and generate a net profit of $100,000."

Funding Request:

Template: Details about your funding requirements, sources of funding, and how the funds will be used.

Example: "XYZ Company is seeking $500,000 in funding to support our initial startup costs, product development, marketing efforts, and operational expenses. We are open to equity investment, convertible notes, or venture debt financing, and are willing to negotiate terms with potential investors. The funding will be used to hire additional personnel, expand our marketing efforts, and accelerate product development to capitalize on market opportunities."

Appendices:

Template: Additional information and supporting documents, such as market research reports, resumes of key team members, legal documents, and contracts.

Example: "Appendix A: Market Research Report - Summary of findings from our market research studies, including industry trends, customer insights, and competitor analysis. Appendix B: Team Bios - Resumes and profiles of our core team members, highlighting their qualifications, experience, and contributions to the company. Appendix C: Legal Documents - Copies of relevant legal documents, such as articles of incorporation, operating agreements, and intellectual property filings."

Chapter 5: Financial Considerations

Budgeting and financial planning are essential aspects of managing a business's finances effectively. Here's a detailed discussion on both topics:

Budgeting:

1. Importance of Budgeting:

Budgeting helps businesses plan and control their finances by allocating resources to various activities and departments.

It provides a roadmap for managing cash flow, controlling expenses, and achieving financial goals.

Budgeting facilitates decision-making by identifying priorities and allocating resources accordingly.

2. Types of Budgets:

Operating Budget: A forecast of revenues and expenses for a specific period, such as a month, quarter, or year.

Capital Budget: A plan for purchasing long-term assets or investments, such as equipment, machinery, or property.

Cash Flow Budget: A projection of cash inflows and outflows to ensure sufficient liquidity for day-to-day operations.

Master Budget: An integrated budget that combines all individual budgets into a comprehensive financial plan.

3. Steps in Budgeting:

Set Goals: Define your financial objectives and priorities, such as increasing revenue, reducing costs, or improving profitability.

Gather Data: Collect relevant financial data, historical performance, market trends, and operational metrics to inform your budget assumptions.

Create Budget Categories: Divide your budget into categories such as sales, expenses, capital expenditures, and cash flow.

Allocate Resources: Determine how much to allocate to each budget category based on your goals, priorities, and available resources.

Monitor and Adjust: Regularly monitor actual performance against budgeted targets and adjust your budget as needed to reflect changing circumstances or priorities.

Financial Planning:

1. Importance of Financial Planning:

Financial planning involves setting goals, evaluating resources, and developing strategies to achieve financial objectives.

It helps businesses anticipate and prepare for future financial needs, opportunities, and challenges.

Financial planning provides a framework for making informed decisions about investments, financing, and risk management.

2. Components of Financial Planning:

Financial Goals: Clearly define short-term and long-term financial objectives, such as revenue targets, profit margins, or market share.

Financial Statements: Prepare and analyze financial statements, including income statements, balance sheets, and cash flow statements, to assess your business's financial health and performance.

Risk Management: Identify potential risks and uncertainties that could impact your business, such as economic downturns, market fluctuations, or regulatory changes, and develop strategies to mitigate or manage these risks.

Investment Strategy: Determine how to allot financial resources to maximize returns and achieve your financial goals, whether through investments in growth opportunities, cost-saving initiatives, or debt reduction.

Tax Planning: Develop tax-efficient strategies to minimize tax liabilities and maximize tax savings, such as taking advantage of tax deductions, credits, or incentives.

Contingency Planning: Establish contingency plans and reserves to handle unforeseen events or emergencies, such as natural disasters, supply chain disruptions, or economic crises.

3. Benefits of Financial Planning:

Provides a roadmap for achieving financial objectives and maximizing profitability.

Helps businesses make informed decisions about resource allocation, investments, and risk management.

Enhances financial transparency and accountability by tracking performance against predefined targets and benchmarks.

Improves financial stability and resilience by anticipating and preparing for future challenges and opportunities.

Funding Options

Exploring funding options is a crucial aspect for aspiring entrepreneurs, especially for those transitioning from unemployment. Here's a breakdown of different funding avenues, including personal savings, loans, and crowdfunding:

Personal Savings:

Utilizing personal savings is often the first source of funding for many entrepreneurs, particularly if they have been saving up for their venture while employed or during periods of financial stability. Advantages of using personal savings include:

Complete control over funds and decision-making.

No interest payments or debt obligations.

Demonstrates commitment and belief in the venture to potential investors.

However, depending solely on personal savings may limit the scale or speed of business growth and could potentially risk personal financial security.

Loans:

Entrepreneurs can access various types of loans to fund their ventures. These may include:

Traditional Bank Loans: Offered by banks and financial institutions, these loans typically require a good credit history and collateral. Interest rates and repayment terms vary.

Small Business Administration (SBA) Loans: Backed by the U.S. Small Business Administration, these loans provide competitive terms and may be easier to qualify for than traditional bank loans.

Online Lenders: Alternative lending platforms offer quick access to funds with less stringent requirements, although interest rates may be higher.

Advantages of loans include access to larger sums of capital, potential for business growth, and establishing creditworthiness. However, entrepreneurs should carefully consider the terms, interest rates, and repayment schedules to avoid overburdening the business with debt.

Crowdfunding:

Crowdfunding platforms enable entrepreneurs to raise funds from a large pool of individuals, typically through online campaigns. There are several types of crowdfunding:

Reward-Based Crowdfunding: Backers contribute funds in exchange for rewards or early access to products or services.

Equity Crowdfunding: Investors receive equity stakes in the business in exchange for their contributions.

Debt Crowdfunding: Entrepreneurs borrow money from backers and repay it with interest over time.

Crowdfunding offers access to capital without the need for collateral or traditional credit checks. It also serves as a marketing tool, allowing entrepreneurs to validate their idea and build a community around their venture. However, running a successful crowdfunding campaign requires significant effort in marketing, storytelling, and campaign management.

Other Funding Sources:

Angel Investors and Venture Capital: High-net-worth individuals or investment firms may provide funding in exchange for equity ownership.

Government Grants and Programs: Governments often offer grants, subsidies, or incentives to support small businesses, particularly in specific industries or regions.

Bootstrapping: Some entrepreneurs choose to bootstrap their ventures, relying on revenue generated from early sales to fund operations and growth.

Tips for managing finances during the startup phase

Managing finances during the startup phase is critical for ensuring the long-term success and sustainability of your business. Here are some tips to help you effectively manage your finances:

Create a Detailed Budget:

Develop a comprehensive budget that outlines all anticipated expenses, including one-time costs (e.g., equipment purchases, initial marketing expenses) and ongoing expenses (e.g., rent, utilities, salaries).

Be realistic in your estimates and account for unexpected expenses by including a buffer or contingency fund in your budget.

Monitor Cash Flow Closely:

Keep a close eye on your cash flow by tracking incoming revenue and outgoing expenses on a regular basis.

Identify patterns and potential cash flow gaps early on to take proactive measures, such as negotiating extended payment terms with suppliers or securing a line of credit.

Prioritize Essential Spending:

Focus your resources on essential expenses that directly contribute to the growth and sustainability of your business.

Differentiate between needs and wants, and avoid unnecessary or extravagant spending during the startup phase.

Minimize Fixed Costs:

Look for opportunities to minimize fixed costs, such as opting for shared office spaces instead of leasing a dedicated office or using cloud-based software instead of investing in expensive hardware.

Consider outsourcing non-core functions, such as accounting or IT support, to reduce overhead costs.

Negotiate Vendor Contracts:

Negotiate favorable terms with vendors and suppliers to secure discounts, bulk pricing, or extended payment terms.

Regularly review supplier contracts to identify opportunities for cost savings or renegotiation.

Bootstrap Where Possible:

Bootstrap your business by relying on personal savings or revenue generated from early sales to fund operations and growth.

Be judicious in seeking external funding to avoid taking on unnecessary debt or diluting equity prematurely.

Invest in Marketing Wisely:

Allocate your marketing budget strategically to channels that offer the highest return on investment for your business.

Experiment with low-cost or free marketing tactics, such as social media marketing, content marketing, and networking, to reach your target audience effectively.

Build a Financial Buffer:

Establish a financial buffer or emergency fund to cover unexpected expenses or periods of low revenue.

Aim to maintain a healthy cash reserve to weather economic downturns or unforeseen challenges.

Seek Professional Advice:

Consider seeking guidance from financial advisors, accountants, or business mentors who can offer insights and expertise in managing startup finances.

Take advantage of free resources and workshops offered by local small business development centers or entrepreneurship organizations.

Review and Adjust Regularly:

Regularly review your financial performance against your budget and strategic goals.

Be prepared to adjust your financial plan and spending priorities as your business evolves and market conditions change.

By implementing these tips and maintaining a disciplined approach to financial management, you can position your startup for long-term success and stability.

Chapter 6: Legal and Regulatory Requirements

Choosing the right business structure is a crucial decision for any entrepreneur, as it impacts various aspects of the business, including taxation, liability, management, and ownership. Here are the most common business structures and their implications:

Sole Proprietorship:

Implications: In a sole proprietorship, the business is owned and operated by a single individual. It's the simplest and most common form of business structure, with minimal legal formalities.

Taxation: Profits and losses are reported on the owner's personal tax return (Form 1040) using Schedule C. The owner is responsible for paying self-employment taxes.

Liability: The owner has unlimited personal liability for the debts and obligations of the business. Personal assets are at risk in the event of lawsuits or business debts.

Management: The owner has complete control over decision-making and management of the business.

Partnership:

Implications: A partnership involves two or more individuals or entities sharing ownership and management responsibilities for the business.

Taxation: Partnerships file an informational tax return (Form 1065) to report profits and losses, but the income "passes through" to the partners' personal tax returns. Each partner pays taxes on their share of the partnership income.

Liability: In a general partnership, partners have unlimited personal liability for the debts and liabilities of the business. Limited partnerships offer limited liability to some partners (limited partners), while general partners retain unlimited liability.

Management: Partners typically contribute to decision-making authority and management responsibilities based on the terms outlined in the partnership agreement.

Limited Liability Company (LLC):

Implications: An LLC is a hybrid business structure that combines the limited liability protection of a corporation with the flexibility and tax advantages of a partnership.

Taxation: LLCs can choose to be taxed as a sole proprietorship/partnership (pass-through taxation) or as a corporation (either as a C corporation or an S corporation). Owners report business profits and losses on their personal tax returns.

Liability: LLC owners (members) have limited personal liability, protecting their personal assets from business debts and liabilities.

Management: LLCs have flexibility in management structure, allowing members to manage the business themselves or designate managers to handle day-to-day operations.

Corporation:

Implications: A corporation is a separate legal entity owned by shareholders. It offers the highest level of liability protection but involves more formalities and regulations.

Taxation: C corporations are subject to double taxation, where the corporation pays taxes on its profits, and shareholders pay taxes on dividends received. S corporations pass corporate income, losses, deductions, and credits through to shareholders for federal tax purposes, avoiding double taxation.

Liability: Shareholders have limited liability, meaning their personal assets are generally protected from business debts and liabilities.

Management: Corporations are managed by a board of directors elected by shareholders. Officers appointed by the board handle day-to-day operations.

Registering a business

Registering a business and obtaining the necessary licenses and permits can vary depending on the location and type of business. Here's a general guide to help readers through the process:

Choose a Business Name:

Select a unique and memorable name for your business.

Check the availability of the chosen name to ensure it's not already in use by another business in your jurisdiction.

Determine the Business Structure:

Decide on the most suitable legal structure for your business, such as sole proprietorship, partnership, LLC, or corporation.

Consider consulting with a legal or financial advisor to understand the implications of each structure on liability, taxation, and management.

Register the Business:

Register your business with the appropriate government authorities, typically the Secretary of State's office or similar agency in your jurisdiction.

Submit the required registration forms, along with any necessary fees.

Provide details such as the business name, address, ownership structure, and contact information.

Obtain an Employer Identification Number (EIN):

If your business has employees or operates as a corporation or partnership, you'll need to obtain an EIN from the Internal Revenue Service (IRS).

Apply for an EIN online through the IRS website or by mail using Form SS-4.

Research and Obtain Licenses and Permits:

Identify the specific licenses and permits required for your business based on its location, industry, and activities.

Conduct thorough research to understand the licensing requirements at the federal, state/provincial, and local levels.

Common types of licenses and permits may include:

Business license or permit: Required to operate a business within a specific jurisdiction.

Professional licenses: Mandatory for certain professions, such as doctors, lawyers, or contractors.

Industry-specific permits: Required for businesses involved in regulated activities, such as food service, alcohol sales, or healthcare.

Zoning permits: Ensures compliance with local zoning regulations for the location of your business.

Complete License and Permit Applications:

Gather the necessary documentation and information required for each license and permit application.

Submit the applications to the relevant government agencies or departments, along with any required fees.

Ensure accuracy and completeness to expedite the processing of your applications.

Renew and Maintain Licenses and Permits:

Keep track of the expiration dates for your licenses and permits to ensure timely renewal.

Stay informed about any changes to regulatory requirements or licensing procedures that may affect your business.

Maintain compliance with all applicable laws and regulations to avoid fines, penalties, or legal consequences.

Consult with Professionals:

Consider seeking guidance from legal advisors, accountants, or business consultants to navigate the registration and licensing process effectively.

Tap into resources provided by government agencies, small business development centers, or industry associations for additional support and information.

By following these steps and adhering to regulatory requirements, you can register your business and obtain the necessary licenses and permits to operate legally and compliantly.

Legal Considerations

Addressing legal considerations such as contracts, intellectual property (IP), and taxes is crucial for protecting your business and ensuring compliance with relevant laws. Here's a breakdown of each aspect:

Contracts:

Contracts are legally binding agreements that outline the rights and obligations of parties involved in a business transaction.

Types of contracts commonly used in business include:

Sales Contracts: Define the terms of sale for goods or services, including price, delivery, and payment terms.

Service Contracts: Specify the scope of work, deliverables, timelines, and compensation for services rendered.

Employment Contracts: Establish the terms and conditions of employment for workers, including roles, responsibilities, compensation, and termination clauses.

Key considerations when drafting or entering into contracts include:

Clearly defining the rights and responsibilities of each party.

Specifying payment terms, deadlines, and conditions for contract termination.

Ensuring contracts comply with relevant laws and regulations, such as consumer protection laws or employment standards.

Reviewing contracts carefully before signing and seeking legal advice if necessary to clarify any ambiguities or potential risks.

Intellectual Property (IP):

Intellectual property refers to creations of the mind, such as inventions, designs, literary and artistic works, trademarks, and trade secrets, which are protected by law.

Types of intellectual property and their protection methods include:

Trademarks: Protect brand names, logos, and slogans from unauthorized use by competitors. Register trademarks with the appropriate government agency to obtain legal protection.

Copyrights: Protect original works of authorship, such as writings, music, and artwork, from unauthorized reproduction or distribution. Copyright protection is automatic upon creation but can be registered for additional legal benefits.

Patents: Protect inventions and innovations from being copied, manufactured, or sold by others. Apply for patents with the relevant patent office to secure exclusive rights for a specified period.

Trade Secrets: Protect confidential information, such as formulas, processes, or customer lists, that provide a competitive advantage to your business. Safeguard trade secrets through confidentiality agreements and security measures.

Conducting IP audits to identify and protect valuable intellectual property assets.

Enforcing IP rights through legal action against infringement or unauthorized use by third parties.

Taxes:

Taxes are mandatory payments imposed by governments on income, sales, property, or other transactions to fund public services and infrastructure.

Business taxes vary depending on factors such as the business structure, location, industry, and revenue.

Common types of business taxes include:

Income Taxes: Paid on profits earned by the business. Sole proprietors and pass-through entities report business income on their personal tax returns, while corporations file separate tax returns.

Sales Taxes: Imposed on the sale of goods or services and collected by businesses on behalf of the government. Rates and regulations vary by jurisdiction.

Employment Taxes: Include payroll taxes withheld from employee wages (e.g., federal income tax, Social Security, Medicare) and employer contributions (e.g., unemployment tax, workers' compensation).

Compliance with tax laws and regulations is essential to avoid penalties, fines, or legal consequences.

Consider consulting with tax professionals or accountants to ensure precise tax reporting and optimization of tax strategies for your business.

By addressing these legal considerations diligently and proactively, you can safeguard your business interests, protect valuable assets, and maintain compliance with relevant laws and regulations.

Chapter 7: Building Your Brand

Branding and positioning are integral components of any successful business strategy, playing crucial roles in shaping how a company is perceived by its target audience and distinguishing it from competitors. Here's a deeper exploration of their importance:

Branding:

Identity and Recognition: Branding encompasses the visual elements, messaging, values, and personality of a business. It creates a distinct identity that helps customers recognize and remember the brand.

Trust and Credibility: Strong branding builds trust and credibility with consumers, as it signals professionalism, consistency, and reliability. A well-established brand inspires confidence and fosters loyalty among customers.

Differentiation and Competitive Advantage: Effective branding sets a business apart from competitors by highlighting its unique selling propositions, such as quality, innovation, or customer service. It creates a competitive advantage that attracts customers and fosters brand loyalty.

Emotional Connection: Brands that resonate emotionally with consumers can create powerful connections and foster long-term relationships. By aligning with customers' values, aspirations, and emotions, branding can evoke positive feelings and influence purchasing decisions.

Brand Equity: Successful branding builds brand equity, which represents the value and goodwill associated with a brand. Brand equity translates into tangible benefits, such as higher perceived value, pricing power, and market share.

Positioning:

Target Audience Focus:

Positioning involves defining how a brand is perceived relative to competitors in the minds of consumers. It requires understanding the needs, preferences, and behaviors of the target audience and crafting a unique value proposition that resonates with them.

Market Differentiation:

Effective positioning highlights the distinct attributes and benefits of a brand that set it apart from competitors. It clarifies why customers should choose your brand over others and communicates a compelling value proposition that addresses their specific needs or pain points.

Relevance and Consistency:

Positioning ensures that the brand message and image are relevant, consistent, and aligned with the needs and expectations of the target market. Consistency across all touch-points reinforces the brand's positioning and reinforces its identity in the minds of consumers.

Adaptability and Flexibility:

Positioning should be adaptable to changes in the market, consumer preferences, and competitive landscape. Brands must continually monitor and adjust their positioning strategies to maintain relevance and effectiveness over time.

Long-Term Growth and Success:

Effective positioning lays the foundation for long-term growth and success by establishing a clear, differentiated identity in the market. It enables brands to carve out a distinctive niche, build customer loyalty, and withstand competitive pressures.

Strategies for creating a strong brand identity

Creating a strong brand identity is essential for building recognition, trust, and loyalty among customers. Here are some strategies to help you establish a compelling brand identity:

Define Your Brand Purpose and Values:

Start by articulating your brand's purpose, mission, and core values. What does your brand stand for? What principles guide your actions and decisions?

Align your brand values with the needs and aspirations of your target audience to create a meaningful connection.

Understand Your Target Audience:

Conduct market research to gain insights into the demographics, psychographics, and behaviors of your target audience.

Understand their needs, preferences, pain points, and aspirations to tailor your brand identity to resonate with them effectively.

Develop a Unique Brand Personality:

Define the personality traits and characteristics that represent your brand, such as friendly, innovative, professional, or adventurous.

Consistently express your brand personality through visual elements, tone of voice, messaging, and interactions with customers.

Craft a Memorable Brand Name and Logo:

Choose a distinctive and memorable brand name that reflects your brand identity and resonates with your target audience.

Design a visually appealing and versatile logo that embodies your brand's personality and values. Ensure it's scalable and suitable for various applications.

Create Consistent Visual Branding:

Establish a cohesive visual identity by defining color schemes, typography, and graphic elements that reflect your brand personality.

Apply your visual branding consistently across all touchpoints, including your website, social media profiles, marketing materials, packaging, and signage.

Develop Compelling Brand Messaging:

Craft clear, concise, and compelling brand messaging that communicates your value proposition, benefits, and differentiation.

Develop a brand story that resonates emotionally with your audience, highlighting your brand's journey, values, and impact.

Deliver Exceptional Customer Experiences:

Focus on delivering exceptional customer experiences at every touchpoint, from initial interaction to post-purchase support.

Consistently uphold your brand promises and values to build trust, loyalty, and advocacy among customers.

Build Brand Awareness Through Marketing and PR:

Implement a strategic marketing and PR strategy to increase brand visibility and awareness.

Utilize various channels and tactics, such as content marketing, social media, influencer partnerships, and public relations, to reach and engage your target audience.

Foster Brand Advocacy and Community:

Encourage brand advocacy by fostering meaningful relationships with customers and stakeholders.

Create opportunities for customer engagement, feedback, and participation to build a loyal community around your brand.

Monitor and Adapt Your Brand Strategy:

Continuously monitor brand performance, customer feedback, and market trends to evaluate the effectiveness of your brand identity.

Be willing to get used to and evolve your brand strategy as needed to stay relevant and competitive in a dynamic marketplace.

Tips for marketing and promoting your business effectively

Effective marketing and promotion are essential for reaching your target audience, generating leads, and driving sales for your business. Here are some tips to help you market and promote your business effectively:

Know Your Audience:

Understand your target audience's demographics, preferences, behaviors, and pain points.

Tailor your marketing messages, channels, and strategies to resonate with your audience effectively.

Create Compelling Content:

Develop high-quality, relevant content that provides value to your audience.

Use a mix of content types, such as blog posts, videos, infographics, and podcasts, to engage and educate your audience.

Utilize Social Media:

Establish a strong presence on relevant social media platforms where your target audience spends time.

Share engaging content, interact with followers, and leverage paid advertising to expand your reach and drive traffic to your website.

Optimize Your Website:

Ensure your website is user-friendly, visually appealing, and optimized for search engines (SEO).

Create informative and compelling landing pages, product/service pages, and calls-to-action (CTAs) to convert visitors into leads or customers.

Implement Email Marketing:

Build and nurture relationships with leads and customers through targeted email marketing campaigns.

Personalize your email content based on recipient preferences, behaviors, and lifecycle stage to improve engagement and conversion rates.

Utilize Search Engine Marketing (SEM):

Invest in pay-per-click (PPC) advertising campaigns to appear prominently in search engine results for relevant keywords.

Optimize your PPC ads for relevance, targeting, and conversion to maximize ROI and drive qualified traffic to your website.

Harness the Power of Influencer Marketing:

Collaborate with influencers or industry experts who have a relevant and engaged audience.

Partner with influencers to create authentic content, endorsements, or reviews that promote your products or services to their followers.

Network and Build Relationships:

Attend industry events, conferences, and networking opportunities to connect with potential customers, partners, and influencers.

Build genuine relationships by offering value, listening to their needs, and being responsive to their feedback.

Offer Promotions and Discounts:

Use promotions, discounts, or special offers to incentivize purchases and attract new customers.

Create urgency and scarcity by setting time-limited or quantity-limited offers to encourage immediate action.

Monitor and Analyze Results:

Track key performance indicators (KPIs) such as website traffic, conversion rates, email open rates, and sales to measure the effectiveness of your marketing efforts.

Use analytics tools to gain insights into audience behavior, campaign performance, and areas for improvement.

Adapt and Iterate:

Continuously evaluate and optimize your marketing strategies based on data and feedback.

Experiment with new tactics, channels, and messaging to stay ahead of competitors and meet evolving customer needs.

By implementing these tips and adopting a strategic approach to marketing and promotion, you can effectively reach and engage your target audience, drive brand awareness and loyalty, and ultimately grow your business.

Chapter 8: Developing Your Product or Service

The process of product or service development involves several stages, from conceptualization to launch and beyond. Here's a detailed overview of each stage:

Idea Generation and Conceptualization:

This initial stage involves generating ideas for new products or services based on market research, consumer insights, industry trends, and internal brainstorming sessions.

Identify opportunities and gaps in the market where your product or service can fulfill unmet needs or solve specific problems.

Refine and prioritize ideas based on feasibility, market demand, potential profitability, and alignment with your business goals and capabilities.

Market Research and Validation:

Conduct thorough market research to validate your product or service concept and understand your target audience's needs, preferences, and pain points.

Analyze competitor offerings, pricing strategies, distribution channels, and customer feedback to identify opportunities for differentiation and competitive advantage.

Gather feedback from potential customers through surveys, focus groups, interviews, or prototype testing to validate demand and refine your concept.

Product Design and Development:

Translate the concept into a tangible product or service through design and development activities.

Collaborate with designers, engineers, and other stakeholders to create prototypes, mock-ups, or wireframes that showcase the features, functionality, and user experience of the product or service.

Iteratively refine and test prototypes based on user feedback, technical feasibility, and performance requirements to ensure alignment with customer expectations and business objectives.

Testing and Quality Assurance:

Conduct comprehensive testing and quality assurance to identify and address any defects, bugs, or usability issues before launch.

Perform functional testing, usability testing, performance testing, and security testing to ensure the product or service meets quality standards and regulatory requirements.

Iterate and refine the product based on testing results to improve reliability, performance, and user satisfaction.

Pricing and Packaging:

Develop pricing strategies and packaging options that reflect the value proposition, positioning, and competitive landscape of the product or service.

Consider factors such as production costs, market demand, perceived value, and pricing sensitivity when determining pricing tiers, discounts, and bundling options.

Design packaging and branding elements that enhance the perceived value and appeal of the product or service and communicate key benefits and features to customers.

Go-to-Market Strategy:

Develop a comprehensive go-to-market strategy that outlines how you will introduce and promote the product or service to your target audience.

Define marketing channels, messaging, and tactics for raising awareness, generating interest, and driving demand among potential customers.

Coordinate cross-functional teams and resources to execute the go-to-market plan effectively and maximize launch success.

Launch and Distribution:

Execute the launch plan and officially introduce the product or service to the market.

Coordinate distribution channels, inventory management, and logistics to ensure availability and timely delivery of the product or service to customers.

Monitor launch performance, gather feedback, and make necessary adjustments to optimize marketing efforts, pricing strategies, and product positioning.

Post-launch Support and Optimization:

Provide ongoing customer support, training, and troubleshooting to address any issues or questions that arise after launch.

Collect and analyze customer feedback, usage data, and market trends to identify opportunities for product improvements, feature enhancements, or expansion into new markets.

Continuously iterate and optimize the product or service based on customer insights and market feedback to maintain competitiveness and drive long-term success.

The importance of customer feedback and iteration

Customer feedback and iteration are integral parts of the product or service development process, playing a crucial role in ensuring that offerings meet the needs and expectations of customers while driving continuous improvement and innovation. Here's why customer feedback and iteration are essential:

Customer-Centricity:

Customer feedback keeps the development process focused on the needs and preferences of the target audience. By listening to customers, businesses can gain valuable insights into their pain points, preferences, and expectations, enabling them to tailor products or services to better meet customer needs.

Validation of Assumptions:

Customer feedback helps validate assumptions made during the initial stages of product or service development. By testing prototypes, concepts, or features with real users, businesses can verify whether their ideas resonate with the intended audience and adjust their approach accordingly.

Identification of Issues and Opportunities:

Customer feedback uncovers potential issues, challenges, or areas for improvement that may not have been apparent during internal development. By listening to customer concerns, businesses can identify usability issues, bugs, or gaps in functionality and take corrective action before launch.

Enhanced User Experience:

Iterating based on customer feedback enables businesses to refine and enhance the user experience, making products or services more intuitive, user-friendly, and enjoyable to use. By incorporating user preferences and addressing pain points, businesses can create offerings that foster greater satisfaction and loyalty among customers.

Competitive Advantage:

Businesses that actively seek and respond to customer feedback can gain a competitive advantage by delivering solutions that better address customer needs and preferences. By continuously iterating based on customer insights, businesses can differentiate themselves from competitors and stay ahead in the market.

Fostering Customer Loyalty:

Engaging customers in the development process and responding to their feedback demonstrates a commitment to customer satisfaction and fosters a sense of loyalty and partnership. Customers appreciate businesses that listen to their input and incorporate their suggestions, leading to stronger relationships and increased brand loyalty.

Innovation and Adaptation:

Iteration based on customer feedback drives innovation and adaptation by encouraging experimentation and refinement. By soliciting feedback early and often, businesses can experiment with new ideas, features, or business models, adapt to changing market dynamics, and stay responsive to evolving customer needs.

Continuous Improvement:

Customer feedback fosters a culture of continuous improvement within the organization, where teams are encouraged to learn from customer interactions, iterate on their offerings, and strive for excellence. By embracing a mindset of continuous improvement, businesses can stay agile, responsive, and relevant in a dynamic marketplace.

Case studies of businesses that successfully developed and launched their offerings

Tesla, Inc.:

Background: Tesla, Inc., founded by Elon Musk in 2003, is a leading electric vehicle (EV) manufacturer and sustainable energy company. Tesla set out to revolutionize the automotive industry by producing high-performance electric cars with long-range capabilities.

Product Development: Tesla's first vehicle, the Roadster, was launched in 2008 as a high-performance electric sports car. Despite initial skepticism about electric vehicles, Tesla focused on developing cutting-edge battery technology, advanced electric drivetrains, and sleek designs to appeal to consumers.

Launch Success: The launch of the Roadster generated significant buzz and attracted attention from early adopters and environmental enthusiasts. Tesla leveraged pre-orders and word-of-mouth marketing to generate demand and build anticipation for its innovative electric cars.

Iterative Improvement: Over the years, Tesla has continued to iterate and improve its product lineup, introducing models such as the Model S, Model X, Model 3, and Model Y, each providing improved performance, range, and affordability. Tesla's focus on continuous innovation, customer feedback, and technological advancement has solidified its position as a leader in the EV market.

Airbnb:

Background: Airbnb, founded by Brian Chesky, Joe Gebbia, and Nathan Blecharczyk in 2008, is an online marketplace for lodging, primarily focused on vacation rentals and short-term stays. Airbnb disrupted the hospitality industry by enabling individuals to rent out their homes or spare rooms to travelers, providing a unique and personalized alternative to traditional hotels.

Product Development: Airbnb started as a way for the founders to monetize their own apartment by renting out air mattresses to attendees of a design conference in San Francisco. Recognizing the potential of their idea, they developed a platform that allowed hosts to list their properties and travelers to book accommodations directly.

Launch Success: Airbnb's launch was fueled by grassroots efforts, with the founders personally reaching out to potential hosts and guests to build the platform's user base. Through strategic partnerships, social media campaigns, and community engagement, Airbnb rapidly expanded its reach and established itself as a trusted platform for travelers seeking unique and affordable accommodations.

Iterative Improvement: Airbnb continuously iterated and expanded its offerings based on user feedback and market demand. The platform introduced features such as enhanced search filters, user reviews, and host verification processes to improve trust and reliability. Airbnb also expanded into new verticals, including experiences and long-term rentals, to cater to diverse customer needs and preferences.

These case studies highlight the importance of innovative product development, strategic launch planning, and iterative improvement in driving the success of businesses across different industries. By focusing on customer needs, leveraging technology, and staying agile, companies like Tesla and Airbnb have been able to disrupt established markets, create value for customers, and achieve sustainable growth.

Chapter 9: Launching Your Business

Launching a business involves several key steps to ensure a successful start and set the foundation for long-term growth. Here's an outline of the essential steps involved in launching a business:

Idea Generation and Validation:

Identify a viable business idea based on market research, industry analysis, and personal interests or expertise.

Validate the idea by conducting market research, assessing demand, and gathering feedback from potential customers or stakeholders.

Business Planning:

Develop a comprehensive business plan outlining your business concept, target market, value proposition, competitive landscape, marketing strategy, operational plan, and financial projections.

Define your business goals, objectives, and key performance indicators (KPIs) to measure success and track progress.

Legal and Regulatory Compliance:

Choose a suitable legal structure for your business, such as sole proprietorship, partnership, LLC, or corporation.

Register your business name, obtain necessary licenses and permits, and comply with local, state/provincial, and federal regulations.

Obtain an Employer Identification Number (EIN) from the IRS (if applicable) and set up tax accounts.

Financing and Funding:

Determine your startup costs and funding requirements, including expenses for equipment, inventory, marketing, and operating expenses.

Explore funding options such as personal savings, loans, grants, crowdfunding, or investment from friends, family, or investors.

Develop a financial plan, including cash flow projections, budgeting, and financial management strategies.

Brand Development:

Define your brand identity, including your brand name, logo, colors, typography, and messaging.

Develop a brand strategy that communicates your unique value proposition, positioning, and personality to your target audience.

Create marketing materials, such as a website, business cards, and promotional materials, to establish a consistent brand presence.

Product or Service Development:

Develop or finalize your product or service offerings, ensuring they meet customer needs, quality standards, and regulatory requirements.

Test prototypes, gather feedback, and iterate based on user input to refine your offerings before launch.

Sales and Marketing Strategy:

Develop a sales and marketing strategy to attract customers, generate leads, and drive revenue.

Identify your target market segments, channels, and tactics for reaching and engaging potential customers.

Implement digital marketing, content marketing, social media, advertising, networking, and other promotional activities to raise awareness and acquire customers.

Operations and Infrastructure:

Set up your business infrastructure, including physical or virtual office space, equipment, technology systems, and operational processes.

Hire and train employees or contractors as needed, and establish workflows and procedures to ensure smooth operations.

Launch Execution:

Plan and execute your business launch, including a launch event or promotional campaign to generate excitement and publicity.

Coordinate logistics, inventory, staffing, and customer service to ensure a successful launch and positive customer experience.

Monitoring and Adaptation:

Monitor key performance metrics, customer feedback, and market trends to evaluate the effectiveness of your launch strategy and make necessary adjustments.

Continuously iterate and optimize your business operations, marketing efforts, and product/service offerings based on real-time feedback and insights.

Guidance on generating buzz and attracting customers

Creating buzz and attracting customers is crucial for launching a business successfully and establishing a strong presence in the market. Here are some effective strategies to help you generate buzz and attract customers:

Create Compelling Content:

Develop high-quality and engaging content that resonates with your target audience. This could include blog posts, videos, infographics, podcasts, or social media posts.

Focus on providing value, solving problems, or entertaining your audience to capture their attention and encourage sharing.

Leverage Social Media:

Build a strong presence on social media platforms relevant to your target audience, such as Facebook, Instagram, Twitter, LinkedIn, or TikTok.

Share engaging content, interact with followers, and participate in conversations to increase visibility, reach, and engagement.

Use hashtags, contests, influencer partnerships, and user-generated content to amplify your message and attract new followers.

Harness the Power of Influencers:

Collaborate with influencers or industry experts who have a large and engaged following in your niche.

Partner with influencers to create authentic content, endorsements, or reviews that promote your brand and offerings to their audience.

Offer Special Promotions or Discounts:

Create limited-time offers, discounts, or promotions to incentivize customers to try your products or services.

Use scarcity and urgency tactics to encourage immediate action and drive conversions.

Host Events or Contests:

Organize virtual or in-person events, webinars, workshops, or product launches to engage with your audience and showcase your offerings.

Run contests, giveaways, or challenges on social media to encourage participation, virality, and brand awareness.

Utilize Search Engine Optimization (SEO):

Optimize your website and content for search engines to improve visibility and attract organic traffic.

Conduct keyword research, optimize meta tags, headings, and descriptions, and create high-quality, relevant content that addresses search intent.

Network and Collaborate:

Build relationships with complementary businesses, industry influencers, local organizations, or community groups.

Collaborate on joint promotions, events, or partnerships to expand your reach, tap into new audiences, and generate mutual referrals.

Encourage Word-of-Mouth Referrals:

Provide exceptional customer experiences and exceed expectations to encourage positive word-of-mouth referrals.

Encourage satisfied customers to share their experiences with friends, family, and colleagues through reviews, testimonials, and social media.

Invest in Paid Advertising:

Allocate a portion of your budget to paid advertising channels such as Google Ads, Facebook Ads, Instagram Ads, or sponsored content.

Target your ads effectively, using demographic, geographic, or interest-based targeting options to reach your ideal customers.

Measure and Analyze Results:

Track key performance indicators (KPIs) such as website traffic, engagement metrics, conversion rates, and sales to evaluate the effectiveness of your marketing efforts.

Use analytics tools to gain insights into customer behavior, identify areas for improvement, and optimize your marketing strategy over time.

Strategies for managing the initial growth phase

Managing the initial growth phase of a business is an exciting yet challenging time, as it involves scaling operations, expanding your customer base, and solidifying your market position. Here are some effective strategies for managing the initial growth phase:

Prioritize Customer Satisfaction:

Focus on delivering exceptional customer experiences to build loyalty and advocacy.

Listen to customer feedback, address concerns promptly, and continuously improve your products or services based on their needs and preferences.

Scale Operations Efficiently:

Assess your current operations and infrastructure to identify areas for improvement and scalability.

Invest in automation, technology, and streamlined processes to increase efficiency, reduce costs, and accommodate growth without sacrificing quality.

Build a Strong Team:

Hire talented individuals who are passionate about your mission and aligned with your company culture.

Delegate responsibilities effectively, empower employees to take ownership, and foster a collaborative and supportive work environment.

Focus on Marketing and Brand Building:

Continue to invest in marketing and brand-building efforts to raise awareness and attract new customers.

Experiment with different marketing channels, tactics, and messaging to identify what resonates most with your target audience.

Monitor Financial Health:

Keep a close eye on your finances and cash flow to ensure stability and sustainability.

Develop and maintain accurate financial projections, budgets, and forecasts to guide decision-making and mitigate risks.

Expand Your Product or Service Offering:

Explore opportunities to diversify your product or service offering to meet the evolving needs and preferences of your target market.

Introduce new features, variations, or complementary offerings that add value and differentiate your business from competitors.

Cultivate Strategic Partnerships:

Identify potential partners, collaborators, or distributors who can help expand your reach and access new markets.

Build mutually beneficial relationships based on trust, shared goals, and complementary strengths to leverage each other's resources and capabilities.

Stay Agile and Adaptive:

Remain agile and adaptable in response to changing market conditions, customer feedback, and competitive pressures.

Embrace a culture of experimentation, innovation, and continuous improvement to stay ahead of the curve and capitalize on emerging opportunities.

Maintain a Customer-Centric Focus:

Keep the needs and preferences of your customers at the forefront of your decision-making process.

Continuously engage with customers, gather feedback, and iterate on your offerings to ensure relevance and satisfaction.

Plan for Long-Term Sustainability:

Balance short-term growth objectives with long-term sustainability and profitability goals.

Develop a clear roadmap and strategy for sustainable growth, taking into account factors such as market dynamics, competitive landscape, and industry trends.

Chapter 10: Overcoming Challenges

Entrepreneurship is a rewarding journey, but it also comes with its fair share of challenges. Here are some common challenges faced by entrepreneurs:

Financial Constraints:

Limited access to capital and funding can hinder the ability to start or grow a business.

Bootstrapping or seeking alternative funding sources such as loans, grants, or crowdfunding may be necessary.

Market Uncertainty:

Navigating volatile market conditions, changing consumer preferences, and competitive landscapes can pose challenges for entrepreneurs.

Conducting market research, staying agile, and adapting quickly to emerging trends are essential strategies for mitigating uncertainty.

Limited Resources:

Entrepreneurs often face constraints in terms of time, manpower, and expertise, especially in the early stages of building a business.

Prioritizing tasks, delegating responsibilities, and seeking outside help or partnerships can help overcome resource limitations.

Customer Acquisition:

Acquiring and retaining customers is a significant challenge for many entrepreneurs, especially in crowded or competitive markets.

Developing effective marketing strategies, building strong relationships with customers, and providing exceptional customer experiences are critical for attracting and retaining customers.

Talent Acquisition and Retention:

Recruiting and retaining top talent can be challenging for startups and small businesses competing with larger companies.

Offering competitive compensation, opportunities for growth and development, and a positive work culture can help attract and retain talented employees.

Regulatory Compliance:

Navigating complex regulatory requirements and compliance issues can be overwhelming for entrepreneurs, particularly in highly regulated industries.

Seeking legal advice, staying informed about relevant regulations, and implementing robust compliance practices are essential for avoiding legal and regulatory pitfalls.

Risk Management:

Entrepreneurship inherently involves risk, including financial, operational, and reputational risks.

Implementing risk management strategies, diversifying revenue streams, and having contingency plans in place can help mitigate risks and protect the business.

Work-Life Balance:

Balancing the demands of running a business with personal commitments and well-being can be challenging for entrepreneurs.

Prioritizing self-care, setting boundaries, and delegating tasks can help maintain a healthy work-life balance and prevent burnout.

Resilience and Persistence:

Entrepreneurship is often marked by setbacks, failures, and unexpected challenges that require resilience and perseverance.

Cultivating a growth mindset, learning from failures, and staying committed to long-term goals can help entrepreneurs overcome adversity and keep moving forward.

Loneliness and Isolation:

Entrepreneurship can be a lonely journey, especially for solopreneurs or those working remotely.

Building a support network of mentors, peers, and fellow entrepreneurs, and seeking opportunities for networking and collaboration can provide valuable support and camaraderie.

By recognizing and addressing these common challenges, entrepreneurs can better navigate the entrepreneurial journey, overcome obstacles, and increase their chances of success. Adaptability, resilience, and a willingness to learn and grow are key attributes that can help entrepreneurs overcome challenges and thrive in the face of adversity.

Practical advice for overcoming obstacles and setbacks

Overcoming obstacles and setbacks is an inevitable part of the entrepreneurial journey. Here's some practical advice to help you navigate challenges effectively:

Maintain a Positive Mindset:

Cultivate a positive attitude and mindset, focusing on solutions rather than dwelling on problems.

Practice gratitude, resilience, and optimism to help you stay motivated and resilient in the face of setbacks.

Seek Support and Guidance:

Don't be afraid to reach out for help and support when facing challenges.

Build a strong support network of mentors, advisors, peers, and fellow entrepreneurs who can offer guidance, advice, and perspective.

Learn from Setbacks:

View setbacks as learning opportunities and opportunities for growth.

Analyze what went wrong, identify lessons learned, and use them to inform future decisions and actions.

Adapt and Pivot:

Be flexible and adaptable in response to changing circumstances and unexpected challenges.

Embrace the concept of "pivoting" if necessary, adjusting your business model, strategy, or approach based on feedback and market conditions.

Break Down Problems:

Break down complex problems or challenges into smaller, more manageable tasks.

Prioritize tasks based on urgency and importance, and tackle them one step at a time.

Stay Organized and Focused:

Maintain clear goals, priorities, and action plans to stay focused and on track.

Use productivity tools, time management techniques, and goal-setting frameworks to help you stay organized and productive.

Take Care of Yourself:

Prioritize self-care and well-being to ensure you have the physical, mental, and emotional energy to tackle challenges.

Make time for rest, relaxation, exercise, and activities that recharge and rejuvenate you.

Stay Persistent and Resilient:

Persistence and resilience are key qualities that will help you overcome obstacles and setbacks.

Stay committed to your goals and vision, and don't let temporary setbacks deter you from pursuing your dreams.

Celebrate Small Wins:

Acknowledge and celebrate small victories and milestones along the way, no matter how small.

Recognizing progress and achievements can boost morale and motivation during challenging times.

Stay Connected to Your Why:

Remind yourself of your purpose, passion, and reasons for pursuing entrepreneurship.

Reconnect with your "why" to stay motivated, inspired, and focused on your long-term goals.

Hug Failure as Part of the Journey:

Understand that failure is a natural part of the entrepreneurial journey and an opportunity for growth.

Embrace failure as a valuable learning experience and use it to become stronger, wiser, and more resilient.

Resilience and perseverance are key traits for success

Resilience and perseverance are indeed essential traits for achieving success in entrepreneurship and any endeavor in life. Here's why they are crucial:

Navigating Challenges:

Entrepreneurship is inherently challenging, with obstacles, setbacks, and failures being common occurrences. Resilience and perseverance enable entrepreneurs to navigate these challenges with determination and tenacity, bouncing back from setbacks and staying focused on their goals.

Overcoming Adversity:

Resilience allows individuals to withstand adversity, setbacks, and failures without giving up or losing hope. Perseverance enables them to keep moving forward despite obstacles, setbacks, or temporary failures, maintaining momentum and progress toward their goals.

Handling Uncertainty:

The entrepreneurial journey is filled with uncertainty and unpredictability. Resilient individuals are better equipped to cope with ambiguity, adapt to change, and navigate uncertain situations with confidence and composure. Perseverance helps them stay the course and remain committed to their vision, even in the face of uncertainty.

Learning from Failure:

Failure is a natural part of the entrepreneurial journey, but resilient individuals view it as a learning opportunity rather than a defeat. They bounce back from failure, analyze what went wrong, and use it as a stepping stone for growth and improvement. Perseverance enables them to keep trying, iterating, and pursuing their goals despite setbacks or setbacks.

Maintaining Motivation and Focus:

Building a successful business requires sustained effort, focus, and motivation over the long term. Resilient individuals possess the mental toughness and emotional fortitude to stay motivated and focused, even when faced with challenges or setbacks. Perseverance helps them stay committed to their goals, pushing through obstacles and staying on track despite setbacks.

Inspiring Others:

Resilient and perseverant entrepreneurs inspire others with their determination, grit, and ability to overcome adversity. By leading by example and demonstrating resilience in the face of challenges, they motivate their team members, partners, and stakeholders to persevere through difficult times and achieve success together.

Achieving Long-Term Success:

Ultimately, resilience and perseverance are key ingredients for achieving long-term success and sustainability in entrepreneurship. They enable entrepreneurs to weather the ups and downs of the journey, adapt to changing circumstances, and persist in the pursuit of their goals, ultimately leading to meaningful achievements and fulfillment.

Chapter 11: Scaling and Growth

Scaling a business involves enhancing its capacity to handle growth while maintaining or improving efficiency, profitability, and customer satisfaction. Here are some strategies for scaling a business effectively:

Develop a Scalable Business Model:

Ensure your business model is designed for scalability from the outset. Focus on creating processes, systems, and infrastructure that can accommodate growth without significant rework or disruption.

Invest in Technology and Automation:

Implement technology solutions and automation tools to streamline operations, improve efficiency, and scale your business processes. This could include customer relationship management (CRM) systems, enterprise resource planning (ERP) software, or workflow automation platforms.

Expand Your Market Reach:

Identify opportunities to expand into new markets, geographies, or customer segments to increase your customer base and revenue streams. This could involve launching new products or services, targeting niche markets, or expanding internationally.

Diversify Your Offerings:

Diversify your product or service offerings to appeal to a broader range of customers and meet different needs or preferences. This could involve introducing new product lines, variations, or complementary services to your existing portfolio.

Optimize Your Marketing and Sales Efforts:

Scale your marketing and sales efforts to reach a larger audience and generate more leads and sales. Invest in digital marketing, content marketing, advertising, and sales enablement strategies to increase brand visibility, attract customers, and drive revenue growth.

Build Strategic Partnerships:

Collaborate with strategic partners, distributors, or resellers to extend your reach and access new markets or customer segments. Forming mutually beneficial partnerships can help you scale more rapidly and efficiently by leveraging each other's resources and networks.

Focus on Customer Success and Retention:

Prioritize customer success and satisfaction to retain existing customers and drive repeat business. Implement customer retention strategies, such as loyalty programs, personalized experiences, and proactive support, to build long-term relationships and maximize lifetime value.

Invest in Talent and Leadership:

Hire and develop a talented team of employees who are aligned with your vision, values, and goals. Invest in training, development, and leadership programs to empower your team to contribute to the company's growth and success.

Manage Cash Flow and Finances:

Monitor and manage your cash flow effectively to support growth initiatives, invest in scaling efforts, and maintain financial stability. Implement sound financial management practices, such as budgeting, forecasting, and managing expenses, to ensure sustainable growth.

Continuously Monitor and Adapt:

Regularly monitor key performance indicators (KPIs), market trends, and customer feedback to assess the effectiveness of your scaling strategies and make necessary adjustments.

Stay agile and adaptable, responding quickly to changing market conditions, emerging opportunities, and potential threats to your business.

Opportunities for expansion and diversification

Expanding and diversifying your business can open up new revenue streams, reach new customers, and reduce risk by spreading your business across multiple markets or product lines. Here are some opportunities for expansion and diversification:

New Geographic Markets:

Explore opportunities to expand your business into new geographic markets, whether regionally, nationally, or internationally.

Conduct market research to identify markets with high demand for your products or services, favorable regulatory environments, and growth potential.

Consider factors such as cultural differences, market saturation, and logistical challenges when expanding into new markets.

New Customer Segments:

Target new customer segments that are underserved or have distinct needs or preferences.

Analyze your existing customer base and identify potential segments to target based on demographics, psychographics, or behavior.

Develop tailored marketing strategies, products, or services to appeal to these new customer segments and differentiate your offerings.

Product Line Extensions:

Extend your product line by introducing new variations, features, or models of your existing products.

Identify opportunities to address different customer needs or preferences, fill gaps in your product portfolio, or capitalize on emerging trends or technologies.

Leverage customer feedback, market research, and competitor analysis to inform product development and ensure alignment with customer expectations.

Complementary Products or Services:

Diversify your offerings by introducing complementary products or services that enhance or supplement your core offerings.

Identify synergies between your existing products or services and related offerings that can create value for customers and drive cross-selling or upselling opportunities.

Partner with other businesses or vendors to offer bundled packages, integrated solutions, or value-added services that appeal to customers . and differentiate your brand.

Vertical Integration:

Consider vertical integration opportunities to expand your business operations upstream or downstream in the supply chain.

Explore options such as backward integration (e.g., acquiring suppliers or manufacturers) or forward integration (e.g., acquiring distributors or retailers) to gain greater control over your value chain, improve efficiency, and capture more value.

Franchising or Licensing:

Franchising or licensing your business model can offer opportunities for rapid expansion with minimal capital investment.

Develop a scalable and replicable business model, standard operating procedures, and training programs to support franchisees or licensees in maintaining consistency and quality across locations.

Ensure strong brand management and support systems to protect brand integrity and ensure franchisee success.

E-commerce and Digital Expansion:

Capitalize on the growth of e-commerce by expanding your online presence and digital capabilities.

Develop or enhance your e-commerce platform, optimize for mobile devices, and leverage digital marketing channels to reach and engage customers online.

Explore opportunities for omnichannel retailing, including click-and-collect, ship-from-store, or in-store pickup options to provide a seamless shopping experience.

International Expansion:

Explore opportunities to expand your business internationally by tapping into global markets.

Conduct thorough market research and feasibility studies to assess market potential, regulatory requirements, cultural considerations, and competitive dynamics in target countries.

Develop localization strategies, adapt your products or services to local preferences and regulations, and build strategic partnerships or distribution channels to support international expansion efforts.

Insights from established entrepreneurs who scaled their businesses

Jeff Bezos, Amazon:

Bezos emphasizes the importance of being customer-centric. He believes that focusing relentlessly on customer satisfaction and continuously innovating to meet customer needs are critical for long-term success.

Bezos also emphasizes the value of experimentation and willingness to fail. He encourages taking calculated risks, experimenting with new ideas, and learning from failures to drive innovation and growth.

Elon Musk, Tesla and SpaceX:

Musk emphasizes the importance of having a bold vision and mission-driven approach. He believes in setting audacious goals that inspire and motivate employees to work towards a common purpose.

Musk advocates for vertical integration and in-house manufacturing to maintain control over product quality, innovation, and cost efficiency. He believes that owning the entire value chain enables greater flexibility and agility in responding to market demands.

Sara Blakely, Spanx:

Blakely emphasizes the value of pliability and perseverance. She faced numerous rejections and setbacks before founding Spanx but remained committed to her vision and persisted despite challenges.

Blakely advocates for embracing failure as a learning opportunity. She believes that failure is an essential part of the entrepreneurial journey and encourages entrepreneurs to view setbacks as stepping stones to success.

Richard Branson, Virgin Group:

Branson emphasizes the importance of delegation and empowering employees. He believes in hiring talented individuals, trusting them to make decisions, and giving them the autonomy to innovate and take risks.

Branson advocates for continuous innovation and disruption. He believes in challenging the status quo, exploring new ideas, and disrupting industries through creativity, experimentation, and unconventional thinking.

Reed Hastings, Netflix:

Hastings emphasizes the value of adaptability and agility. He believes in constantly evolving and adapting to changing market dynamics, consumer preferences, and technological advancements.

Hastings advocates for a culture of freedom and responsibility. He believes in giving employees the freedom to innovate and take ownership of their work while holding them accountable for results.

Indra Nooyi, Former CEO of PepsiCo:

Nooyi emphasizes the importance of diversity and inclusion. She believes that diverse perspectives and backgrounds drive innovation and creativity, leading to better decision-making and business outcomes.

Nooyi advocates for long-term thinking and sustainable growth. She believes in balancing short-term results with a focus on building enduring value and making decisions that benefit all stakeholders, including employees, customers, and society.

These insights from established entrepreneurs highlight the importance of customer focus, innovation, resilience, adaptability, and a strong company culture in scaling a business successfully. By embracing these principles and lessons learned from experienced entrepreneurs, aspiring business owners can increase their chances of achieving sustainable growth and long-term success.

Chapter 12: Conclusion

Here are the key takeaways from the book "From Unemployment to Entrepreneurship":

Mindset Shift:

Transitioning from unemployment to entrepreneurship requires a shift in mindset. Instead of viewing unemployment as a setback, see it as an opportunity to pursue your passion, create your own path, and take control of your future.

Starting Small:

You don't need to have everything figured out from the beginning. Start small, take incremental steps, and focus on making progress each day. Embrace experimentation, learning, and iteration as you navigate the entrepreneurial journey.

Funding Options:

Explore various funding options, including personal savings, loans, crowdfunding, or investment from friends and family. Consider what works best for your situation and business needs, and be resourceful in securing the necessary capital to get started.

Financial Management:

Effective financial management is essential during the startup phase. Develop a budget, track expenses, and manage cash flow diligently to ensure sustainability and avoid financial pitfalls.

Business Structures and Legal Considerations:

Understand different business structures and their implications, such as sole proprietorship, partnership, LLC, or corporation. Register your business, obtain necessary licenses and permits, and comply with legal and regulatory requirements.

Branding and Positioning:

Invest in branding and positioning to differentiate your business and create a strong identity in the market. Define your brand values, personality, and messaging to resonate with your target audience and stand out from competitors.

Product Development and Customer Feedback:

Focus on developing products or services that solve a specific problem or address a customer need. Gather feedback from early adopters, iterate based on user input, and continuously improve your offerings to meet customer expectations.

Marketing and Promotion:

Develop a marketing strategy to reach and engage your target audience effectively. Utilize digital marketing, social media, content marketing, and networking to raise awareness, attract customers, and drive sales.

Scaling and Growth:

As your business grows, explore opportunities for expansion and diversification. Consider entering new markets, introducing new products or services, or forming strategic partnerships to scale your business and increase revenue streams.

Resilience and Perseverance:

Entrepreneurship is a journey filled with challenges and setbacks. Cultivate resilience and perseverance to overcome obstacles, stay focused on your goals, and keep pushing forward, even in the face of adversity.

Dear Reader,

Are you feeling stuck in a rut, unsure of what the future holds? Perhaps you've recently experienced unemployment, and the uncertainty of what comes next is weighing heavily on your shoulders. But let me tell you something: amidst the challenges and setbacks lies an opportunity waiting to be seized.

Now is the time to embark on an extraordinary journey - the journey of entrepreneurship. It's a path filled with twists and turns, highs and lows, but one that offers endless possibilities for growth, fulfillment, and success.

Don't let fear or doubt hold you back. Instead, channel that energy into taking the first step towards your dreams. Start by envisioning the life you want to create for yourself - the impact you want to make, the legacy you want to leave behind.

Believe in your ideas, your abilities, and your resilience. Remember that every successful entrepreneur was once faced with uncertainty and adversity, but they chose to persevere, to innovate, to create something meaningful out of nothing.

You have unique talents, experiences, and insights that the world needs. Your ideas have the power to solve problems, inspire change, and make a difference. But none of it will happen unless you take action.

So, what are you waiting for? Seize this moment, this opportunity, to turn your dreams into reality. Embrace the challenges, learn from the setbacks, and celebrate the victories along the way.

Surround yourself with mentors, advisors, and fellow entrepreneurs who will support and encourage you on your journey. Seek knowledge, seek guidance, but above all, trust in yourself and your ability to overcome any obstacle that comes your way.

The road ahead may be long and challenging, but it's also filled with infinite possibilities and opportunities for growth. Embrace the journey, embrace the adventure, and most importantly, embrace the incredible potential within you to create a life and a legacy that you're proud of.

The world is waiting for your brilliance, your passion, your unique contribution. Don't keep it waiting any longer. Take that first step, and let your entrepreneurial journey begin.

With belief, determination, and a relentless pursuit of your dreams, there's no limit to what you can achieve.

Here's to you, the fearless entrepreneur, and the extraordinary journey that lies ahead.

Go forth and conquer.

Warm regards,

Asit Saha

Here are some resources for further learning and support to help aspiring entrepreneurs on their journey:

Online Courses and Platforms:

Udemy: Offers a wide range of courses on entrepreneurship, business development, marketing, and more.

Coursera: Provides courses from top universities and institutions on topics such as entrepreneurship, innovation, and business strategy.

LinkedIn Learning: Offers video courses taught by industry experts on various business and entrepreneurial topics.

Books:

"The Lean Startup" by Eric Ries: Offers practical advice for building and scaling a startup by applying lean principles and continuous innovation.

"Start with Why" by Simon Sinek: Explores the importance of purpose and vision in entrepreneurship and building a successful business.

"The $100 Startup" by Chris Guillebeau: Provides insights and case studies of entrepreneurs who built successful businesses with minimal resources.

"Zero to One" by Peter Thiel: Explores the principles of innovation and entrepreneurship, offering valuable insights for building a unique and successful business.

Podcasts:

"How I Built This" by NPR: Features interviews with entrepreneurs and business leaders who share their stories of building successful companies.

"The Tim Ferriss Show": Hosted by entrepreneur and author Tim Ferriss, this podcast features interviews with top performers in various fields, including entrepreneurship, business, and personal development.

"The GaryVee Audio Experience" by Gary Vaynerchuk: Offers insights and advice on entrepreneurship, marketing, and building a personal brand from entrepreneur and marketing expert Gary Vaynerchuk.

Networking and Communities:

Meetup: Provides a platform to find and join local groups and events related to entrepreneurship, startups, and business networking.

Startup Grind: Hosts events, workshops, and networking opportunities for entrepreneurs and startup founders in cities around the world.

Reddit: Join subreddits such as r/Entrepreneur, r/startups, and r/smallbusiness to connect with other entrepreneurs, ask questions, and share insights and experiences.

Incubators and Accelerators:

Y Combinator: Offers a startup accelerator program and resources for early-stage entrepreneurs, including funding, mentorship, and access to networks.

Techstars: Provides accelerator programs, mentorship, and resources for tech startups and entrepreneurs.

Startup Weekend: Hosts events where aspiring entrepreneurs can pitch ideas, form teams, and launch startups in just 54 hours.

Business Support Organizations:

Small Business Administration (SBA): Offers resources, training, and support for small businesses and entrepreneurs in the United States.

SCORE: Provides free mentoring, workshops, and resources for small business owners and entrepreneurs.

Chambers of Commerce: Local chambers of commerce often offer networking events, workshops, and resources for small businesses and entrepreneurs in their communities.

Appendix: Additional Resources

Here are some worksheets, checklists, and tools that can be referenced throughout the book "From Unemployment to Entrepreneurship":

Business Plan Template:

A comprehensive template to help entrepreneurs outline their business idea, target market, competitive analysis, marketing strategy, financial projections, and more.

Market Research Worksheet:

A worksheet to guide entrepreneurs through the process of conducting market research, including identifying target customers, analyzing competitors, and assessing market trends and opportunities.

Financial Projections Spreadsheet:

A spreadsheet template to help entrepreneurs create financial projections for their business, including sales forecasts, expense estimates, cash flow projections, and break-even analysis.

Marketing Plan Checklist:

A checklist to help entrepreneurs develop a marketing plan, including defining target audience, setting marketing objectives, selecting marketing channels, creating messaging and content, and measuring results.

Startup Costs Checklist:

A checklist to help entrepreneurs estimate and plan for startup costs, including one-time expenses (e.g., equipment, licenses, initial inventory) and ongoing expenses (e.g., rent, utilities, payroll).

Legal and Compliance Checklist:

A checklist to help entrepreneurs ensure compliance with legal and regulatory requirements, including business registration, permits and licenses, tax obligations, intellectual property protection, and employment laws.

Customer Feedback Survey Template:

A survey template to gather feedback from customers, including satisfaction levels, product or service preferences, suggestions for improvement, and likelihood to recommend.

Sales Pipeline Tracker:

A spreadsheet or tool to track sales leads and opportunities through the sales pipeline, including stages (e.g., prospecting, qualification, proposal, closing) and status updates.

SWOT Analysis Worksheet:

A worksheet to conduct a SWOT analysis (Strengths, Weaknesses, Opportunities, Threats) to assess the internal and external factors affecting the business and inform strategic planning.

Goal Setting Worksheet:

A worksheet to help entrepreneurs set SMART (Specific, Measurable, Achievable, Relevant, Time-bound) goals for their business, including short-term and long-term objectives.

Networking Tracker:

A spreadsheet or tool to track networking activities, contacts, follow-ups, and outcomes to build and maintain relationships with mentors, advisors, customers, and partners.

Here is a list of recommended books, websites, and organizations for further exploration in entrepreneurship:

Books:

"The Lean Startup" by Eric Ries: Offers insights into lean principles and methodologies for building and scaling startups in a fast-paced, uncertain environment.

"Zero to One" by Peter Thiel: Explores the principles of innovation and entrepreneurship, offering valuable insights for building unique and successful businesses.

"Start with Why" by Simon Sinek: Discusses the importance of purpose and vision in entrepreneurship and building a successful business.

"The $100 Startup" by Chris Guillebeau: Provides insights and case studies of entrepreneurs who built successful businesses with minimal resources.

"Good to Great" by Jim Collins: Examines what it takes for companies to transition from being good to great and sustain long-term success.

Websites:

Entrepreneur.com: Offers articles, resources, and guides on various aspects of entrepreneurship, including starting a business, marketing, finance, and leadership.

Inc.com: Provides business news, insights, and resources for entrepreneurs and small business owners, including articles, videos, and tools.

StartupGrind.com: Hosts events, workshops, and resources for entrepreneurs and startup founders, including interviews with successful entrepreneurs and thought leaders.

FastCompany.com: Covers innovation, technology, leadership, and entrepreneurship, offering articles, insights, and inspiration for aspiring entrepreneurs.

TED.com: Features TED Talks on a wide range of topics, including entrepreneurship, leadership, creativity, and innovation, from thought leaders and experts around the world.

Organizations:

Small Business Administration (SBA): Offers resources, training, and support for small businesses and entrepreneurs in the United States, including financing options, business counseling, and government contracting assistance.

SCORE: Provides free mentoring, workshops, and resources for small business owners and entrepreneurs, including one-on-one mentoring sessions with experienced business professionals.

Young Entrepreneur Council (YEC): A community of young entrepreneurs under 45 years old, offering networking opportunities, resources, and peer-to-peer support for aspiring and established entrepreneurs.

National Association for the Self-Employed (NASE): Provides resources, advocacy, and support for self-employed individuals and small business owners, including access to healthcare, tax benefits, and business resources.

Startups.co: Offers a suite of tools and resources for entrepreneurs, including business planning software, funding resources, and a community of startup founders and experts.

These books, websites, and organizations offer valuable insights, resources, and support for aspiring entrepreneurs at every stage of their entrepreneurial journey. Whether you're just starting out or looking to scale your business, exploring these resources can provide inspiration, guidance, and practical advice to help you achieve your entrepreneurial goals.

Don't miss out!

Visit the website below and you can sign up to receive emails whenever Asit Saha publishes a new book. There's no charge and no obligation.

https://books2read.com/r/B-A-WRTEB-STVAD

BOOKS 2 READ

Connecting independent readers to independent writers.

Did you love *From Unemployment to Entrepreneurship: A Guide to Starting Your Own Business*? Then you should read *Mastering Sales: Strategies for Winning Deals*[1] by Asit Saha!

[2]

"Mastering Sales: Strategies for Winning Deals" is a comprehensive guide designed to empower sales professionals with the knowledge, skills, and strategies needed to achieve excellence in the art of sales. Written for both newcomers and seasoned veterans alike, the book covers a wide range of topics essential for success in today's competitive marketplace.

The book begins by laying a solid foundation for sales mastery, exploring fundamental principles such as understanding customer needs, effective communication, and building trust and rapport. Readers are then guided through each stage of the sales process, from prospecting and lead generation to negotiation and closing. Along the way, practical

---

1. https://books2read.com/u/mdYgAd

2. https://books2read.com/u/mdYgAd

strategies and techniques are provided to help navigate common challenges and obstacles encountered in the sales journey.

Emphasizing the importance of strategic selling, the book delves into advanced techniques for identifying and qualifying leads, uncovering customer pain points, and tailoring solutions to meet specific needs. Readers learn how to effectively overcome objections, handle rejections, and navigate the closing process with confidence and finesse. Proven strategies for negotiation and building long-term relationships with clients are also explored in detail.

Throughout the book, readers encounter real-world case studies and examples that illustrate key concepts and demonstrate how they can be applied in practice. Each chapter includes actionable insights to help readers reinforce their learning, apply new techniques, and track their progress. Additionally, expert advice, tips, and best practices from seasoned sales professionals are provided to inspire and empower readers on their sales journey.

"Mastering Sales: Strategies for Winning Deals" is not just a book; it's a comprehensive guide and indispensable resource for anyone seeking to achieve mastery in the art of sales. Packed with practical strategies, actionable techniques, and expert advice, this book empowers readers to unlock their full potential, secure winning deals, and achieve unparalleled success in the competitive world of sales.

About the Author

Writes to motivate and entertain.